Hippos
and
Rhinos

Joanne Mattern

ROurke
Educational Media
rourkeeducationalmedia.com

Teacher Notes available at
rem4teachers.com

www.rourkeeducationalmedia.com

PHOTO CREDITS: Cover: ©; Title Page: © Patrick Rolands, Gvision; Page 2-3: © Carlos Caetano; Page 4: © Evelyn Peyton, Mhpiper; Page 5: © tunart, Pauline S Mills, Mark Stay, edge69; Page 6: © Creative Commons; Page 7: © Creative Commons, Matthijs van Schendelen; Page 8: © Creative Commons; Page 9: © Musser Remy, Sattapapan Tratong; Page 10: © Michel de Nijs; Page 11: © Lantapix, Kitchner Bain; Page 12: © Wendy Nero; Page 13: © Dean Bertoncelj; Page 14: © Steve Geer, Myerscw; Page 15: © Irina88w; Page 16: © Smellme, TheBiggles, pop_jop; Page 17: © S100apm, Nico Smit; Page 18: © rusm, kevdog818; Page 19: © Steffen Foerster, Henri Faure; Page 20: © Steven Wynn; Page 21: © Fernando2148, Science and Society; Page 22: © Creative Commons;

Edited by Precious McKenzie

Cover Design by Renee Brady
Interior Design by Cory Davis

Library of Congress PCN Data

Hippos and Rhinos / Joanne Mattern
(Eye to Eye with Animals)
ISBN 978-1-61810-117-4 (hard cover) (alk. paper)
ISBN 978-1-61810-250-8 (soft cover)
Library of Congress Control Number: 2011944408

Rourke Educational Media
Printed in the United States of America,
North Mankato, Minnesota

Rourke
Educational Media

rourkeeducationalmedia.com
customerservice@rourkeeducationalmedia.com • PO Box 643328 Vero Beach, Florida 32964

Table of Contents

Chapter 1

Lumbering Land Animals

Hippos and rhinos are two of the heaviest animals that walk on planet Earth. A full-grown hippo weighs at least 3,300 pounds (1,500 kilograms), but many weigh a lot more. Some hippos have been measured at more than 9,000 pounds (4,080 kilograms). That's a lot of hippo!

Rhinos are supersized too. The heaviest rhinos weigh about 8,000 pounds (3,630 kilograms). Rhinos are the second largest land animals. Only the elephant is bigger. Both rhinos and hippos can be very dangerous to people. If you startle one of these big animals, they are likely to attack!

Hippopotamus

Rhinoceros

Hippopotamus

WHAT'S YOUR NAME?

The words hippo and rhino are nicknames. The full names of these big beasts are hippopotamus and rhinoceros.

Rhinoceros

MAN: Average Height 6 ft. (2 meters)
HORSE: Average Height 5 ft. (1.5 meters)
RHINO: Average Height 5 ft. (1.5 meters)
HIPPO: Average Height 5.2 ft. (1.6 meters)
AFRICAN ELEPHANT: Average Height 11.5 ft (3.5 meters)

3.5 m
3.0 m
2.5 m
2.0 m
1.5 m
1.0 m
0.5 m
0 m

Chapter 2
Ancient Beasts

Hippos and rhinos have lived on Earth for millions of years. Hippos have been around for more than 25 million years. Scientists found **fossils** of ancient hippos in Asia. In 2004, scientists discovered ancient hippo fossils in coastal Great Britain. Scientists did not know ancient hippos lived that far north.

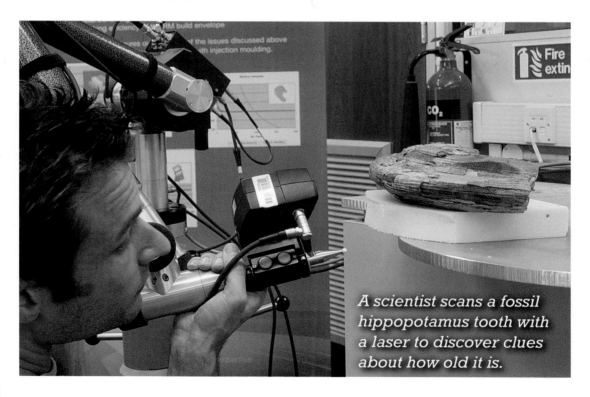

A scientist scans a fossil hippopotamus tooth with a laser to discover clues about how old it is.

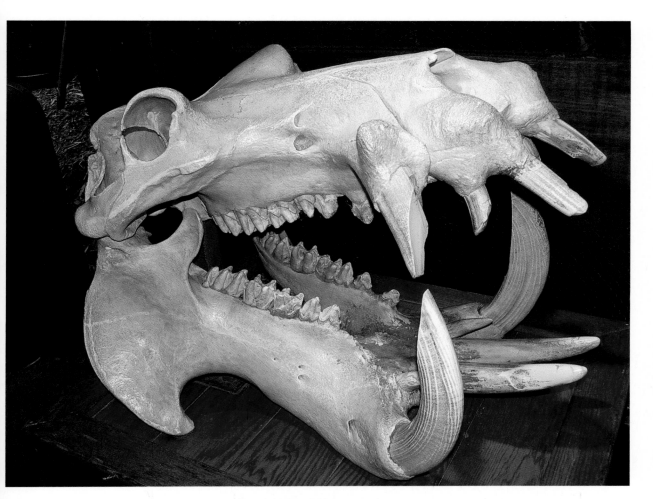

FUN FACT

Ancient hippos were even larger than the hippos we know today. The hippo fossils found in Great Britain could have belonged to hippos that were two to three tons larger than modern hippos.

Rhinos have been on Earth even longer than hippos. Fossils show that rhinos have been around for about 35 million years. Scientists discovered fossilized remains of a woolly rhino in the Himalayas. This rhino had a large, flat horn which scientists think it used to push snow out of its way when it looked for vegetation to eat.

This skeleton of an ancient rhinoceros shows just how large its horn was!

Both hippos and rhinos got their names from the ancient Greeks. The word hippopotamus comes from two Greek words that

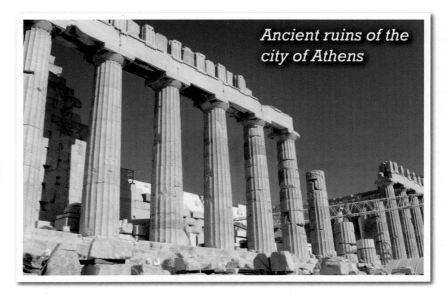
Ancient ruins of the city of Athens

mean *river horse*. The ancient Greeks may have picked that name because hippos are large and they are such good swimmers.

The rhinoceros's name also describes what it looks like. In Greek, *rhino* means *nose* and *ceros* means horn. The rhino's horn is not a hard bone at all. It is made out of **keratin**.

Hippos, with their large bodies and tremendous jaws, are some of the deadliest animals on the planet.

9

Chapter 3
Life as a Hippo

Hundreds of years ago hippos lived all over Asia, Africa, and Central America. Over the years, hippos in Asia and Central America died out because there wasn't enough land or food to support them. People farmed the land around rivers and lakes, leaving little food and **habitat** for hippos. People would kill hippos that damaged their crops. Today, the only place hippos live in the wild is in Africa.

There are two kinds of hippos, river hippos and pygmy hippos. The river hippo lives in **grasslands** near water. Pygmy hippos live in the West African rainforest. It is very hot and wet there.

WHERE IN THE WORLD?

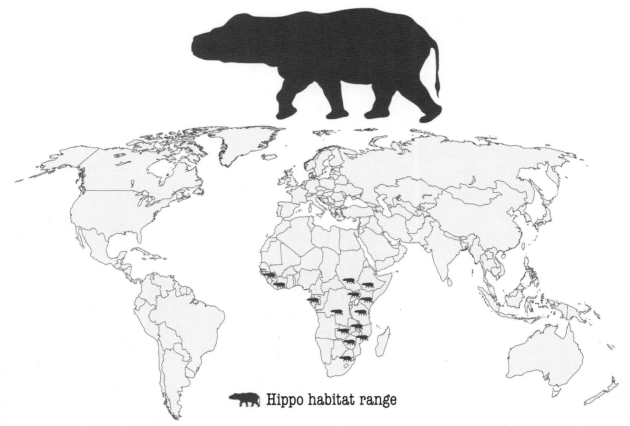

Hippo habitat range

A MINI-HIPPO

Pygmy hippos are smaller than river hippos. They only weigh about 600 pounds (275 kilograms). Pygmies are also a lot more shy. While river hippos live in large **herds**, pygmy hippos live alone or in groups of two or three.

11

Hippos are **herbivores**. They only eat plants. Hippos are **nocturnal**. That means they sleep during the day. At night, the herd of hippos leaves the water to **graze** on grass and leaves. Hippos travel the same well-worn path night after night. They usually graze by themselves for about five hours and then return to the hippo path, slipping back into the water before daylight.

If hippos can not find enough vegetation to eat they will migrate as far as 24 to 30 miles (40-60 km) in search of food.

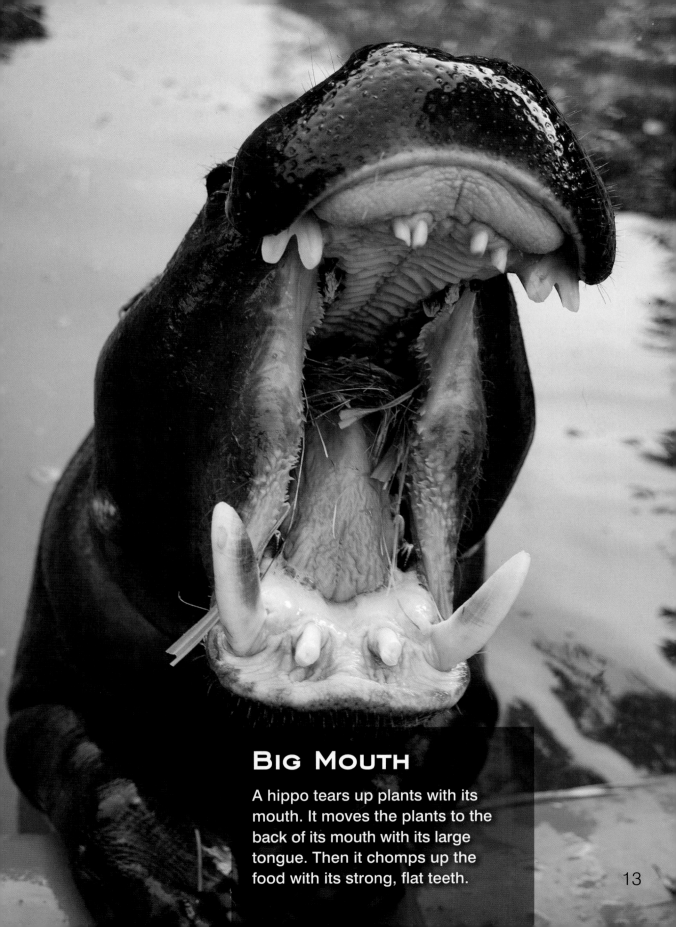

BIG MOUTH

A hippo tears up plants with its mouth. It moves the plants to the back of its mouth with its large tongue. Then it chomps up the food with its strong, flat teeth.

A hippo's body is large and strong. These animals have thick skin, but their skin is very **sensitive**. Hippos lay in the water and mud to keep cool. The mud also keeps away biting insects. When a hippo gets too warm or too dry, its mucous glands **secrete** a red, oily fluid. That oil keeps the hippo moist. It also keeps it from getting sunburned and its insect bites from getting infected!

FUN FACT

Scientists call the oily fluid "blood sweat" because it looks like the hippo is sweating blood. A hippo has no real sweat glands, so this layer of mucus is the best way the animal can keep cool when it is out of the water.

DIVING CHAMP

A hippo can stay under water for up to five minutes before it needs to come to the surface to breathe. This allows them to play games with one another in the water and helps them avoid threats.

Chapter 4
Reigning Rhinos

Rhinoceroses live in Africa and Asia. Black and white rhinos live in Africa. These are the most common types of rhino.

Black rhino

White rhino

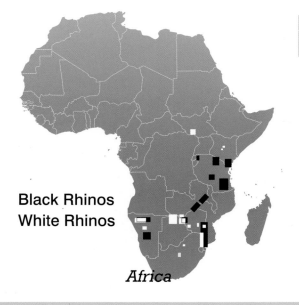

Black Rhinos
White Rhinos

Africa

Indian Rhino
Sumatran Rhino
Javan Rhino

Asia

WHERE THEY LIVE MAP

- ■ Black Rhinos—eastern and southern Africa
- □ White Rhinos—eastern and southern Africa
- Indian Rhino—northeast India and Nepal
- Sumatran Rhino—Vietnam, Malaysia, Indonesia
- ■ Javan Rhino—Vietnam, Malaysia, Indonesia

Most rhinos live in grasslands or forests. They eat leaves and grass. Some rhinos, like the black rhino, eat leaves, branches, and small trees. Rhinos pull food into their mouths with their strong lips. White rhinos eat 27-37 pounds (60-80 kg) of vegetation a day, sometimes more!

Did You Know?

Rhinos only drink water one or two times a day but they drink 170 pints (80 liters) at a time!

A rhino can have one or two horns. These horns are made of keratin. That's the same material your fingernails are made of and other animal hooves are made of. A rhino's horn looks like a weapon. Sometimes the animal does use it for self defense. Most of the time, a rhino uses its horn to dig dirt or guide its young.

White Rhinoceros

Indian Rhinoceros

Rhinos look like they are wearing steel plates! A rhino's skin is thick and tough and it protects them from predators and the sharp, thick underbrush in their habitat. Rhinos like to wallow in the mud. The mud protects them from sun, insects, and heat.

Rhinos have weak eyesight. They rely on their sense of smell to warn them of danger.

A bird called the oxpecker is a great friend to rhinos! An oxpecker sits on a rhino's back and eats ticks, fleas, and other insects that crawl on the rhino's skin. The bird gets a good meal and the rhino stays itch-free!

Chapter 5
Big Beasts in Danger!

Hippos and rhinos are both **endangered**. Rhinos are hunted for their horns. People in Korea, China, and Malaysia think rhino horns can be used as medicine. Others value the horn for its beauty and they make jeweled daggers out of rhino horn. Hippos were hunted for their teeth and skin. People called **poachers** kill rhinos and hippos and sell their bodies for money.

More than 450 rhinos were killed by poachers in Africa in 2011, despite efforts to protect them.

This rhino may have lost its horn to a poacher who wanted to sell it or make it into medicine.

Did You Know?

Yemeni men value rhino horn dagger handles as symbols of their manhood. In China, people have used rhino horns as ornaments since the seventh century. Rhino horns were made into ceremonial cups, buttons, and even paperweights.

Most hippos and rhinos live in wildlife **preserves**.
You can also see them in zoos around the world.
Zoos and wildlife preservation societies are working
hard to protect hippos and rhinos so that they do not
become extinct.

Glossary

endangered (en-DAYN-jurd): in danger of dying out

fossils (FAH-suhlz): remains of an animal or plant from millions of years ago

grasslands (GRASS-landz): areas covered with grass and without tall trees

graze (GRAZE): to eat grass and other plants

habitat (HAB-uh-tat): the place where an animal lives

herbivores (ER-buh-vorz): animals that only eat plants

herds (HURDZ): large groups of animals

keratin (KEH-ruh-tin): a hard material that makes up a rhino's horn

nocturnal (nok-TUR-nuhl): active at night

poachers (POH-churz): people who hunt protected animals

preserves (prih-ZERVZ): places where animals can live safely in the wild

secrete (suh-CREET): to ooze a liquid

sensitive (SEN-suh-tiv): easily damaged

Index

Websites To Visit

nationalgeographic.com/kids/animals/mammals/hippopotamus

animal.discovery.com/mammals/rhinoceros

www.sandiegozoo.org/animalbytes/t-rhinoceros.html

About the Author

Joanne Mattern has written hundreds of nonfiction books for children. She really loves learning about wild animals, so writing HIPPOS AND RHINOS was a lot of fun for her! Joanne grew up on the banks of the Hudson River in New York state and still lives in the area with her husband, four children, and an assortment of pets that does not include any hippos or rhinos.

Ask The Author!
www.rem4students.com